When God Steps In

When God Steps In

Claiming Divine Resources
for Life's Desperate Situations

by

A.B. Simpson

CHRISTIAN PUBLICATIONS
Camp Hill, Pennsylvania

Christian Publications, Inc.
3825 Hartzdale Drive, Camp Hill, PA 17011

Faithful, biblical publishing since 1883

ISBN: 0-87509-590-9
LOC Catalog Card Number: 95-83823
© 1997 by Christian Publications, Inc.
All rights reserved
Printed in the United States of America

97 98 99 00 01   5 4 3 2 1

When God Steps In
was formerly published under the title
But God

CONTENTS

Preface

The subject of this little book is the greatest in the world. "I have lost everything," said a sorrowing woman to us once, "everything but God." That one phrase seemed to loom like a whole heaven and eclipse all that she had lost, for if she had God she had lost nothing and had gained everything.

The greatest need of our age and of every age, the greatest need of every human heart, is to know the resources and sufficiency of God.

The apostle paints it like a rainbow across a black and stormy sky. After describing the lost and helpless condition of sinful men, dead in trespasses and sin, children of wrath, subjects of the prince of the powers of the air, he suddenly pauses and utters the two words, "But God, who is rich in mercy, for his great love wherewith he loved us, Even when we were dead in sins, hath quickened us together with Christ." (Ephesians 2:4–5, KJV).

Paul again gives us the key to the true life of holiness in his short but striking antithesis, "I no longer live, but Christ lives in me" (Galatians 2:20).

The words stand out as the key to God's providence as we read the story of Peter's imprisonment and his approaching doom, while Herod waited to bring him forth to execution. Then follows that simple significant sentence. "But the church was earnestly praying to God for him" (Acts 12:5). And that little "but" was mightier than Herod's wrath or the Pharisees' hate or the bars and bolts of the prison.

Awfully and solemnly the same words loom up and again in the parable of the fool who had staked all on this world's wealth and fortune. He had consulted everybody else about his pleasures and his plans until suddenly, like the cold gates of death and judgment, we come against the terrible sentence, "But God said to him, 'You fool!' " (Luke 12:20).

This book is an attempt to unfold the all-sufficient and infinite variety of the resources of God. We will look at the times when God stepped into situations with His resources and won the victory.

CHAPTER
1

The God of Elijah and Elisha

"Where now is the LORD, the God of Elijah?"
(2 Kings 2:14)

I have always been glad that Elisha did not say, "Where is Elijah?" He had lost his friend and spiritual father, and if ever a sense of bereavement could have been justified, it would have been in the case of Elisha. But his only thought was of the Master and not of the servant. Back of all of Elijah's marvelous life and work, he saw only the infinite resources of that God that could be as much to him as He had been to his master. The deep cry of his soul was not for mere human sympathy, but for the manifestation of God's supernatural power and presence. The deep need of Elisha's life was the same deep need that every earnest soul feels today—the revelation of God, the realization of the supernatural.

Elisha was thinking of all that God had been to Elijah and was longing that He might be the same

1

to him. Oh, that our hearts might have the same longing to know the God of Elijah, the God of Elisha!

The God of Elijah

How much Jehovah had been to the servant whom He had just translated into His glorious presence! Suddenly called from the solitudes of Gilead, this strange, lonely man, whose life and character had been molded amid the majesty of nature alone with his God, was immediately projected into the very midst of an age of unparalleled wickedness and a scene of godless culture and luxury.

The beautiful capital of the kingdom of Israel was under the dominion of wicked King Ahab. And his conduct and scepter were wholly under the control of the infamous woman whose name has ever since stood as the symbol of every kind of evil—Jezebel, the Sidonian idolatress.

Single-handed, the prophet of Gilead was called upon to fight the combined forces of a wicked court, a mercenary and idolatrous priesthood, and a whole people who had turned from the way of godliness and sunk either in sin or heartless apathy. The situation would have been a desperate one but for the resources of God. With a faith that never faltered but once, the mighty prophet met the emergency and claimed the fullness of his divine equipment. At his word the heavens were sealed and the harvest withered. And at the same word the treasures of rain were opened and the earth gave forth her fruit. During the drought the ravens of the wilderness ministered to him, and the widow's little supply of meal and oil was multiplied until the months of famine had gone.

At last all Israel was gathered at his command for a mighty convocation on Mount Carmel. There he stood alone to vindicate the name of Jehovah against the wicked Jezebel, the angry Ahab, the eight hundred prophets of Baal and the myriads of Israel. The altar was prepared, the trenches were dug and filled with water. The vain attempts of the heathen prophets were repeated again and again and only met with ignominious failure. Then the final momentous test was uttered and the power of the Omnipotent summoned to send the heavenly fire. Quick as the lightning flash it fell, devouring the sacrifices and licking up the floods that filled the trenches. It blazed before the wondering gaze of the assembled myriads until their intense emotion could hold back no longer. Thundering from that mighty court the shout went up, echoing from Carmel's rocky vales, "The LORD—he is God! The LORD—he is God!" (1 Kings 18:39).

Swiftly the victory was followed in its awful finish. The prophets of Baal were slain before the reaction had time to come. Then, bending in agonized prayer before his God, the prophet claimed, as the climax of the whole wondrous scene, the opening heavens and the descending rain. Girding his loins like some great leader, in mighty triumph he ran before the chariot of Ahab to the entrance of the palace gates while the torrents fell. The nation rejoiced that the judgment was passed and soon the hearts of the people turned back again.

Let us glance at some of these representative scenes.

1. God's Resources

Looking back to the last days of Elijah and the transition of his ministry to his successor, we are struck at the very first illustration of God's resources. It is wonderful the way Jehovah chooses His agents and supplies the worker that He most needs at every emergency and crisis in the history of His kingdom. Elijah had just failed and fled from Jezebel in the supreme moment of his triumph. Too elated, perhaps, the reaction had come before he was prepared to withstand it, and so that humiliating chapter is written in the story of his life, "Elijah was afraid and ran for his life" (19:3).

But how tenderly God dealt with him! He let him run till he was thoroughly tired out. He let him rest under the juniper tree, and awoke him again and again and again, ministering to his hunger and weariness, until the tired prophet was rested and refreshed. And then God sent him to Horeb that He might give him His last commissions. One of these commissions was a release from the work of which, for a moment, he allowed himself to grow tired, and with it the appointment of those that were to succeed him. "Go back the way you came, and go to the Desert of Damascus," was the Lord's message. "When you get there, anoint Hazael king over Aram. Also, anoint Jehu son of Nimshi king over Israel, and anoint Elisha son of Shaphat from Abel Meholah to succeed you as prophet" (19:15-16).

How swiftly he was excused. How soon his successor was elected! How easy it is for God to go through the court of a sinful kingdom or to the farm and field where some humble Elisha is following the oxen and the plough, and call for the instrument He needs just at the moment He requires him. Oh, how humbling it is to our self-importance and pride! God does not need any voice, and it is just an honor and a privilege that He lets us serve Him. Let us be very careful how we get tired too soon or ask to be relieved. God may take us at our word, and He has plenty of others to fill our place.

2. Picking an Instrument

Second, we have another illustration in First Kings 22:34 of how easy it is for God to pick out an instrument, even an unconscious instrument, for His work and plan. Long before He had decreed and announced the punishment of Ahab for his crimes, His longsuffering had waited and spared the wicked king again and again. At last the judgment came, but the means were most solemn in their simplicity. Ahab was just returning from the battlefield where he had escaped the assaults of the foe and was securely riding in his chariot away from harm and danger. But "someone drew his bow at random" (22:34), and the arrow sped from the bow, the sender neither knowing nor caring where it went. At that very moment by a slight movement the joints of Ahab's coat of mail were opened at the very spot which that arrow struck. It entered and pierced him to the heart, and he cried, "Wheel around and get me out of the fighting. I've been wounded" (22:34). As the sun sank in the west, his life ebbed away and the judgment long threatened was at last fulfilled.

How easy it is for God to strike His foes. How little we need to worry and trouble ourselves about our enemies! "Do not take revenge, my friends, but leave room for God's wrath, for it is written: 'It is mine to avenge; I will repay,' says the Lord" (Romans 12:19).

3. *Jehovah's Power*

But even greater than this was the revelation of Jehovah's power in the life of Elijah. To him it was permitted, before any other messenger of Jehovah, to burst open the very gates of death itself and summon back the departed spirits from the unseen world. When his work was done, a yet higher triumph awaited him; for he himself was raised even beyond the touch of death and was carried to the heavenly world with horses and chariots of fire.

The Lord God of Elijah is the God of life and death, the God of earth and heaven, the God of nations and princes and kings, the God of nature and grace, the God of judgment and retribution, the God who is a consuming fire, mightier than all the forces of nature, of man, of earth, of hell. This mighty God, whose working Elisha had witnessed in the life of his master and whose presence he claimed as he went forth, proved His infinite resources in a life yet more wonderful than even Elijah's had been.

The God of Elisha

Elisha's was a larger life than even Elijah's. Elijah, the prophet of fire, was a more startling figure and, perhaps, reached at times a higher flight than his successor. Yet Elisha's sphere took a broader sweep and reached a plane nearer to humanity at large and more helpful to the ordinary man and woman.

I would suggest that you take a single week and every day read a chapter for seven successive days. Start with the second chapter of Second Kings, read to the seventh, and then conclude on the seventh day with the 13th chapter, which gives the last scenes in his closing life. Such a review will bring God nearer to your conceptions. It will awaken in you the intense desire for such a life and walk with Him, and often prompt the cry and prayer, "Where now is the LORD, the God of Elijah?" (2 Kings 2:14).

1. Removing Difficulties

The God of Elisha is the God who can remove the most formidable difficulties from our pathway. The moment Elisha had received the promised power of the Spirit of God, he was met, not by hands of welcoming angels, but by the swelling tide of the angry Jordan. It refused to allow him to pass over to the field of his future ministry, where the critical young students of Bethel were watching to see what kind of a prophet he was. But with a single cry, "Where now is the LORD, the God of Elijah?" he smote the waters and called upon the same almighty resources. The floods divided and the angry torrent became an escort to open the way to the other side. And as he marched across in triumph, the critical students, awed and humbled, bowed at his feet and humbly said, "The spirit of Elijah is resting on Elisha" (2:15).

The very first thing that you and I will meet when we take some new hold of God for power and blessing will probably be a swollen Jordan, an overwhelming obstacle. What are you going to do about it? There is nothing you can do but remember what God can do and turn at once from your strength and weakness, from your doubts and difficulties, and take Him for your all-sufficiency. Your cry will be, "What are you, O mighty mountain? Before [the God of Elisha] you will become level ground" (Zechariah 4:7).

2. *Control of Nature*

The God of Elisha is able to control the forces of nature. In Second Kings 2:20 and 4:42, there are two fine examples of the power of God through His servant Elisha in the natural world. The first was the healing of barren soil by the sprinkling of some salt into the spring of waters.

And the second was the multiplying of the bread by which the hunger of a hundred men was satisfied from twenty little buns, even as in later ages on the Galilean shore the five thousand were fed by the Master's miracle.

And we still have a God who can help us on the farm, in the kitchen, who can fertilize our field, protect our crops, send our harvest, give us our daily bread, multiply the little which the housewife has until it becomes an ample store for her little family circle. So God is walking today with many a humble saint in the lowly place of toil and trial.

3. God of Emergencies

The God of Elisha is a God of emergencies. The third chapter of Second Kings tells us the story of the water famine in the valley of Eden and the wonderful deliverance which came through Elisha. "This is what the LORD says" was the prophet's answer to the unbelief of Joram and the fears of Jehoshaphat. "You will see neither wind nor rain, yet this valley will be filled with water, and you, your cattle and your other animals will drink. This is an easy thing in the eyes of the LORD; he will also hand Moab over to you" (3:17-18).

The God of Elisha can send water when there is neither wind nor rain nor any outward sign. He can give us help when, like Jehoshaphat, we are even in a place where we should not be. It is an easy thing for Him to do the greatest thing for those who trust Him. His resources are so super-

abounding that we never can exhaust them. And
what He does for us is but a loving provocation
for us to ask Him to do yet more.

4. *Grace and Temporal Blessing*

The God of Elisha is the God of grace as well as
of temporal blessing. The fourth chapter of Second Kings gives the incident of the widow's oil
and the wonderful deliverance it wrought for her.
As she poured it into the empty vessels, it multiplied and grew until it became a fortune, enough
to pay her debt and keep her all her days. The oil,
we know, was the symbol of the Holy Spirit. The
deep lesson is, that if we have the Holy Spirit in
our hearts and in our houses, He will become the
source of every needed supply and the guarantee
of every possible blessing.

All we need is to use what we have and to take
the trials and needs that come to us as empty vessels into which He will pour His fullness and
transform every difficulty into an occasion of
blessing and praise.

5. *Health and Healing*

The God of Elisha is the God of health and
healing. There is no finer example of God's provi-
sion for our physical diseases than the story of
Naaman and his healing in the waters of Jordan. It
was not Elisha that healed him, for he refused
even to touch him. It was simply the power of
God coming to the suffering one the moment he
trusted and obeyed. His washing in the Jordan

was but the consummated act of faith that met God exactly on His Word and persevered in the attitude of faith until the blessing fully came. The same God still waits to heal all that come to Him in the same patient, persistent and overcoming faith.

6. *God of the Supernatural*

The God of Elisha is the God of the supernatural. The incident of the sixth chapter of Second Kings is a fine illustration of the principle of the supernatural.

Going down with his college boys to build the log college on the banks of the Jordan, one of the students lost his axhead in the water. The prophet met the emergency by commanding the iron to swim, thus showing that the power of God is superior even to the laws of nature. This is just what the resurrection and ascension of Jesus Christ prove and make practicable for us also. We still have the God who can rise above even His own laws when the interest of His children requires it. He is "head over everything for the church, which is his body, the fullness of him who fills everything in every way" (Ephesians 1:22-23).

Where Is He?

Where is the Lord God of Elijah and Elisha? He is wherever His people's need requires the manifestations of His presence and His power. In the darkest times and the most sinful age He is still what He was in the age of Jezebel and Ahab.

He is the God not of a few exclusive people and transcendent circumstances, but He is the God who, as in the case of Elisha, will meet us in the palace, on Mount Carmel, or in the battle, at the plough, or with the widow in her little cottage. He will meet us anywhere and everywhere that need can claim and faith can trust Him.

Elisha was a man of the people and his life teaches us that our Christ is the Christ of the common people still. His promise and His grace are for every situation and every suffering child. He is where faith can trust Him, prayer can wait for Him, and patience can hold fast until He comes. This God is our God, the God and Father of our Lord and Savior Jesus Christ, "the same yesterday and today and forever" (Hebrews 13:8). *Lord, help us to understand You better and to trust You more.*

CHAPTER
2

The God of Paul

And my God will meet all your needs according to his glorious riches in Christ Jesus. (Philippians 4:19)

This is Paul's legacy to his disciples and friends. He bequeaths to us his God and all that his own life and experience have revealed of His infinite all-sufficiency. This wonderful phrase begins with "God" and ends with "Christ Jesus," and between these two extremes lie, first, "all your needs," and second, "his glorious riches." It is not only a banknote, but it is a whole bank with all the resources of the proprietor behind it.

The greatest need of Christian life is to know God and His resources. And the Bible is just a revelation of the all-sufficiency of God through the human channels and instruments that He has used to reveal Himself. The typical lives and characters of the Holy Scriptures are not so much remarkable for themselves as for the divine Presence that stands behind each of them. The difference between human heroes and sacred characters lies just in this: The man is just a man, but behind the man of God, God Himself is ever standing greater than the man and overshadowing him by His infinite and glorious Presence.

Behind the Man

When one of the greatest of our national heroes returned, his grateful country crowned him with the honors of a successful war. Behind him there stood, of course, the valuable realm that he had conquered for us and the glorious flag which he represented. But that was all. And he himself was for the time the supreme personality that absorbed the public eye and heart. But behind Enoch is Enoch's God. Behind Elijah is Elijah's God. Behind Moses is a Presence far mightier than Moses. Behind Paul is the marvelous Presence that his life revealed. His last will and testament bequeaths his God to every Christian heart.

Standing on the threshold of his new life, and just awaking from the startling farewell of his glorified master, Elisha faced the flowing Jordan and the mighty tasks of his divine ministry. But we are so glad that he did not ask for Elijah. He asked for Elijah's God.

Paul was separated from his beloved Philippian friends. But he does not try to comfort them with the mere promise of his earthly presence, for he knew that even that could be temporary. Rather, he gives them his God. Compressing into a single sentence all the meaning of his own experience and of God's infinite riches he says: "My God will meet all your needs according to his glorious riches in Christ Jesus" (4:19).

Each of these representative lives reveals God in some new light, and so Paul's God stands before us in a light as distinctive and quite as glorious as Elisha's or Elijah's. What are the lessons the life of Paul teaches us about the all-sufficiency of God? We have often looked at Paul, now let us look at Paul's wonderful God.

A God Who Saves

First, we see that the God of Paul is a God who can save the greatest sinner and reach the hardest case of unbelief. Paul presents himself to us as the pattern sinner. With deepest humility, and yet utmost self-unconsciousness, he tells us not how deserving he was, but how unworthy. He counts himself the pattern sinner set forth on purpose to show that God can save anybody since He saved him. "For that very reason," he says, "I was shown mercy so that in me, the worst of sinners, Christ Jesus might display his unlimited patience as an example for those who would believe on him and receive eternal life" (1 Timothy 1:16). If Paul could be saved, anybody could be.

The peculiarity of Paul's case, that made it especially difficult, was that Paul was not so much a bad sinner as a good one. He was a moral man, a righteous man, a blameless man, a conscientious man, a religious man, a most earnest worker for the religious cause in which he believed. There was no loose joint in his harness where the arrow of conviction could enter. He had lived before God "in all good conscience" (Acts 23:1), unto the day of his conversion. Such a man is very difficult to reach. Our appeals roll off like water. God's severest warnings found no lodging place in his armor-plated soul.

Yet one flash of Christ's revealing light, one glimpse of His suffering face and pitying love, broke this hard and willful soul to pieces and sent him forth to live under the constraining power of grateful love. Are you praying for some hard case, some godless, hardened soul? Remember the God that saved Paul and pray and not faint.

Raise Us to Sainthood

Second, the God of Paul is able to raise us to the highest saintliness, for Paul is not only a pattern sinner, but he is also a pattern saint. He dares to say, "Whatever you have learned or received or heard from me, or seen in me—put it into practice" (Philippians 4:9).

The primary feature of his saintliness is that it is all Christlikeness. He never stands in front but always hides behind the form and loveliness of Jesus Christ. He never tells us of his perfections, but only of the grace of his Savior. The very watchword of his life is: "I have been crucified with

Christ and I no longer live, but Christ lives in me" (Galatians 2:20). This is the highest as well as the lowliest form of holy character. If we could impress people with the fact that we are preeminently holy, we would discourage them, for they would put their own lives in contrast and say they could never reach us. But if we tell them of a life conscious of its weakness that was able to take from Another the strength it did not have, the righteousness it could not work out, the loveliness that was foreign to its nature, and that that gracious One will be the same to them that He has been to us, then people are encouraged and lifted up.

The story of Paul's spiritual experience is a constant revelation of Jesus and His nearness to, and sufficiency for the weakest heart, the humblest saint, the most strangely constituted and severely tried and hindered life. Three things were especially marked in Paul's saintliness. The first was what we might call righteousness, the quality of integrity, that essential foundation of all deeper and higher experience: a life right with God and men.

But that was not all. There was a second higher quality of Christian sweetness and loveliness. In one of his most striking passages he contrasts the righteous man with the good man. The righteous man is like the granite rock, hard but yet true. But the good man is like the moss-covered mountainside, radiant with flowers and fresh with springing cascades, beautiful as well as true. "For a good man," he says, "someone might possibly dare to die," but for the righteous man "very rarely" (Romans 5:7) would one die.

Now Paul exhorts us to combine these two elements. "Whatever is right" he speaks of in one clause. "Whatever is lovely" (Philippians 4:8), in another, and he bids us combine them. In his own life they were beautifully blended. His holiness was not harsh, inaccessible, unattractive, but full of lowliness, gentleness, affectionateness, sympathy and consideration for others. Being simple as a child, loving as a woman, tender as a mother, affectionate as a father, having a fountain of tears always ready to flow at a touch, a heart all throbbing with humanness as well as holiness—this is the life that wins and draws many, and it will come from a higher source, from the heart of Jesus. It was Paul who wrote about love and lived it, too, but he might well have put the word "Christ" wherever he put "love" in the thirteenth chapter of First Corinthians.

But there was a third element in the character of Paul for which Christ was equally sufficient, and that is the practical element, the element of sense, sound judgment, symmetry and balance of character. "God [has given] us," he says, "a spirit of power, of love and of self-discipline" (2 Timothy 1:7). It was this wonderful completeness that gave strength to every part of Paul's extraordinary life. Now the God who made him what he was, is waiting to be the same to each of us if we will meet the tests and take Him at His word.

Strength in Suffering

Then the third element of the God of Paul is His ability to strengthen in times of suffering. Paul was not only a pattern sinner and pattern saint, but a pattern sufferer. In one of the most remarkable passages of his letters he speaks of himself as a "spectacle" (1 Corinthians 4:9), and a "gazingstock" (Hebrews 10:33, KJV), and one set forth in the eye of the universe to exhibit what God can be in human life.

He was exposed to the severest trials that can come to a human soul or body. Listen to the list in Second Corinthians:

Five times I received from the Jews the forty lashes minus one. Three times I was beaten with rods, once I was stoned, three times I was shipwrecked, I spent a night and a day in the open sea, I have been constantly on the move. I have been in danger from rivers, in danger from bandits, in danger from my own countrymen, in danger from Gentiles; in danger in the city, in danger in the country, in danger at sea; and in danger from false brothers. I have labored and toiled and have often gone without sleep; I have known hunger and thirst and have often gone without food; I have been cold and naked. Besides everything else, I face daily the pressure of my concern for all the churches. Who is weak, and I do not feel weak? Who is led into sin, and I do not inwardly burn?

If I must boast, I will boast of the things that show my weakness. (11:24-30).

Again we have a description almost as startling in First Corinthians.

> For it seems to me that God has put us apostles on display at the end of the procession, like men condemned to die in the arena. We have been made a spectacle to the whole universe, to angels as well as to men. We are fools for Christ, but you are so wise in Christ! We are weak, but you are strong! You are honored, we are dishonored! To this very hour we go hungry and thirsty, we are in rags, we are brutally treated, we are homeless. We work hard with our own hands. When we are cursed, we bless; when we are persecuted, we endure it; when we are slandered, we answer kindly. Up to this moment we have become the scum of the earth, the refuse of the world. (4:9-13)

Here he tells us that, as in the Roman games, the brutal master of ceremonies reserved for the last a bloody tragedy, and, after men's lives had been played with through the day, at last the thirst for blood was glutted and some noble gladiator was given over to be murdered in the arena.

So he says, "God has put us apostles on display at the end of the procession, like men condemned to die in the arena" (4:9). Then he speaks of every form of privation, suffering and distress. Of all that can come from physical drudgery, the deprivation of friends and life, the cruel desertion of loved friends, the fury of the elements, the perils of the sea, the hate of Satan, and the inner burdens that came to him for the sake of others through his sympathetic nature. Paul bore, as it were, the whole burden of the suffering body of Christ. And it seemed as though it were appointed for him to endure that which remained of the afflictions of Christ for His body, the Church.

Yet how did he go through the fiery ordeal? Not only did he endure it, but he was more than conqueror. Not only did he stand it with patience, but he gloried in it with triumphant joy. Listen to him as he cries:

We are hard pressed on every side, but not crushed; perplexed, but not in despair; persecuted, but not abandoned; struck down, but not destroyed. We always carry around in our body the death of Jesus, so that the life of Jesus may also be revealed in our body. (2 Corinthians 4:8-10)

Listen to him again.

Known, yet regarded as unknown; dying, and yet we live on; beaten, and yet not

killed; sorrowful, yet always rejoicing; poor,
yet making many rich; having nothing, and
yet possessing everything. (6:9-10)

Listen to him once more as he tells the elders of
Ephesus not only of what he has suffered but that
the Holy Spirit has delivered him. "In every city
the Holy Spirit warns me that prison and hardships are facing me." (Acts 20:23) And yet what
does he add: "None of these things move me
(20:24, KJV)." They did not even disturb him nor
take away his strength from the needs of others
and the claims of his work. "I consider my life
worth nothing to me, if only I may finish the race
and complete the task the Lord Jesus has given
me—the task of testifying to the gospel of God's
grace" (20:24).

What was the secret of this wonderful patience,
this victorious suffering? He tells us in another
place how God answered him when he asked that
the great burden of suffering be removed. The answer was, " 'My grace is sufficient for you, for my
power is made perfect in weakness.' Therefore I
will boast all the more gladly about my weak-
nesses, so that Christ's power may rest on me.
That is why, for Christ's sake, I delight in weakness, in insults, in hardships, in persecutions, in
difficulties. For when I am weak, then I am
strong" (2 Corinthians 12:9-10).

These things became to him but vessels to hold
more of his Lord's grace. So he not only endured
them, but welcomed them and turned everything

into victory and praise through the all-sufficient grace of Jesus Christ.

Sustains the Suffering Body

Then, in the fourth place, the God of Paul is a God that can strengthen and sustain the suffering body. Paul's experience reveals two phases. The first is the direct healing of actual sickness by the immediate manifestation of the power of God in the body. We read of one of these healings in Second Corinthians 1:8-10. Here we are told of a case where he was "under great pressure, far beyond [his] ability to endure, so that [he] despaired even of life" (1:8). But God delivered him in direct answer to prayer.

We are told of another similar incident in Acts, where he had been apparently stoned to death at Lystra. But as the disciples stood around him he rose to his feet. He then went quietly on with his work as though nothing had happened.

But we have a second phase of divine life in Paul, revealed in the fourth chapter of Second Corinthians. "We always carry around in our body the death of Jesus, so that the life of Jesus may also be revealed in our body. . . . Therefore we do not lose heart. Though outwardly we are wasting away, yet inwardly we are being renewed day by day" (4:10, 16). This was not so much an immediate act of healing as a constant habit of drawing the life of Jesus Christ directly from Him. Paul found this life of Jesus a constant experience in his mortal flesh, enabling him to rise above the power of his own natural weakness and go through life with a weak frame and yet a supernatural strength. The same God can still be the same to us in our mortal flesh as well as in our spiritual life.

Sufficient for Service

Finally, the God of Paul is sufficient for all the service that He claims from us. Paul's life was pre-eminently one of service. "I worked harder than all of them," he could say, and yet he added, "yet not I, but the grace of God that was with me" (1 Corinthians 15:10).

He took the strength of Jesus and the Holy Spirit for every task and he counted himself equal to anything in this divine enduement. Indeed, every situation that came to him was but an opportunity for service. If he was in prison, he immediately went to work for the salvation of all the prisoners. If he was joined to two soldiers in the barracks, before morning they were converted, and writing to the Philippians from Rome he told them the joyful news that all that are in the barracks have accepted Jesus Christ. Look at him on his voyage to Rome. We see a missionary who started off for the greatest field in the world. Having received a free pass as a prisoner of the law, he took command of the ship through that awful tempest, first saving the lives and then the souls of all on board. Look at him again at Rome brought before the emperor, and even dragged into the Colosseum to fight with the lions. How did he look at it? It was simply an opportunity for service.

There he had, at last, a chance to preach to old bloody Nero the message of judgment and salvation. Forgetting all about his own danger and even unconscious for the time of the roar of the Numidian lion waiting perhaps to devour him, his thought was to be true to his trust and let God take care of him. Writing about this incident he says: "At my first defense, no one came to my support, but everyone deserted me. . . . But the Lord stood at my side and gave me strength, so that through me the message might be fully proclaimed" And he adds: "I was delivered from the lion's mouth" (2 Timothy 4:16-17). His business was to preach to Nero; God's business was to look out for the lion.

In the face of a thousand disadvantages with neither churches nor missionary boards to back him, in a single lifetime this marvelous man carried the gospel to all the leading cities of the world. He planted the churches from which all the Christianity on earth today has come down. What was the secret of it all? "My God," and "his glorious riches in Christ Jesus" (Philippians 4:19).

Friend, will you have Paul's God? Will you use His infinite resources for such a life of saintliness, victorious suffering and holy service as his was?

CHAPTER
3

The God of Jacob

"Do not be afraid, O worm Jacob."
     (Isaiah 41:14)

"I, the LORD, *am your Savior,*
     your Redeemer,
the Mighty One of Jacob."
          (49:26)

What a combination! The worm Jacob, the Mighty One of Jacob! A worm united to Omnipotence! What is so weak and worthless as a worm! What is so mighty as the mighty One of Jacob! This tells the story—not Jacob, but Jacob's God; not man, but the all-sufficient God displacing man and substituting His own infinite fullness.

We have seen a little of the resources of God in the story of Elijah and Elisha and in the life of Paul. But someone might say that all this might well occur in lives so lofty and sublime, but can I,

27

a weak and worthless man, reach such heights of victory and glory?

Therefore we turn now to the life of a weak and worthless man that we may show that God uses such men to make them the peculiar illustrations of His own grace and sufficiency. The one lesson of Jacob's life is sovereign grace. We have already seen that this was one lesson of Paul's life and that his deepest thought and highest testimony was "I no longer live, but Christ lives in me" (Galatians 2:20).

If ever there was a man who deserved to be called a worm, it was the supplanting son of Isaac. And yet this was the man whom God selected from among all the patriarchs to be head of Israel's tribes and the real founder of the covenant people to whom were committed the oracles of God. Therefore Jacob is more especially fitted to set forth the grace of God than any other of the Bible characters. Let us look at the lessons which his life illustrates with respect to the resources of our God.

Unworthy and Unattractive Lives

We see in Jacob's life the God who can choose and see unworthy and unattractive lives and characters. Had we been choosing on natural principles between the two sons of Isaac, we may have preferred the big-hearted, impulsive Esau. His father did prefer him and tried his best to hold for him the tribal blessing and divine birthright.

There was little naturally in Jacob that was attractive. Jacob was intensely selfish and deceitful, disposed to take advantage of another's misfortune. There is no type of human nature that, by the common consent of mankind, is more detestable than the hard, cold, heartless miser. He is lower even than the groveling sensualist in the scale of humanity. And yet God chose this man in order that there is no class of humanity so hard, so hopeless, as not to be within reach of sovereign grace, indeed, that God loves a hard case and that "where sin increased, grace increased all the more" (Romans 5:20).

If there is a soul reading these lines who is discouraged about himself, remember Jacob, and then remember Jacob's God, the One who could choose a worm and make him a prince with God and with men. He is still saying, "God chose the foolish things of the world to shame the wise; God chose the weak things of the world to shame the strong" (1 Corinthians 1:27).

Sees the Possibilities

The God of Jacob is a God who can discern elements of good and possibilities of the highest things in the most unlikely lives. Behind Jacob's meanness there was something that had in it inherently the elements of power and blessing, and behind Esau's apparent nobility there was something earthborn and incapable of the highest things. Not without reason has God said of these two men, "Jacob I loved, but Esau I hated" (Romans 9:13).

What was it in Jacob that God loved and that became a point of contact with His grace? It was that element which we might call the spiritual. It was the peculiar insight into the higher things which discerns and chooses the best. It is a kind of intuition, a spiritual instinct, the germ in fact, of the higher nature. It enabled Jacob to discover, to appreciate, and to desire intensely all that was meant in the divine birthright, while on the other hand the lack of it led Esau to despise this.

All Esau cared for was the gratification of his natural and grosser appetites. He was a splendid animal; that was all. When he was hungry, he wanted food, and he cared not how he got it. He had not the power to comprehend or prize the higher blessing which was his by natural right. In the hour of his extremity we find him exclaiming, "Look, I am about to die. . . . What good is the birthright to me?" (Genesis 25:32). That was the very time when it should have meant most to him, for it secured to him the favor of his covenant God, a part among the covenant people. It would secure the high honor of standing in the front of that line that was to lead up to the promised seed, the coming Messiah. While it had the highest natural dignities and privileges connected with it, it was preeminently spiritual in its meaning and value. And yet Esau, realizing none of these things, recklessly and blindly threw it away for a mess of pottage. The sacred writer crystallizes into a single sentence the meaning of the act, "So Esau despised his birthright" (25:34).

God loved in Jacob the quality that appreciated, desired and chose the higher things. God loved him for it and God came to meet him and gave him what he desired. "They have received their reward in full" (Matthew 6:2), is the awful sentence of Christ on humanity. Men and women generally get what they want. If they are after earthly things they will probably find them. If they "seek first his kingdom and his righteousness, . . . all these things will be given to [them] as well" (6:33). "[They who] hunger and thirst for righteousness, . . . will be filled" (5:6).

It is often true that the worst and the best are closely akin in human nature. The most discouraged and sinful man is often so because the devil has seen his folly and has perverted the bud into a thorn. God sees everything through the crust of evil and he comes to meet and satisfy the yet undimmed jewel of some deep and earnest longing for better things. It is comforting to know that we have a God who is not looking for the evil in us. He is looking for the good that is trying to find some point of contact with better things, that is looking in every human soul for some place where the chain of mercy can fasten and lift us to the skies.

Friend, if you are far away from God and conscious of utter unworthiness, I would ask you: Would you have God's love for your heart? Would you choose His will if it were offered to you? Would you part with everything to have the best and highest things? Then you have that which God loved in Jacob and that which will feel after God until it finds Him.

Reveals Himself to the Ignorant

In the third instance, we see in Jacob's God one who can reveal Himself to a soul that is utterly ignorant of Him. When Jacob went out from his father's house and his mother's arms he had indeed set his heart on the highest things so far as he knew them and won by a very unworthy transaction the covenant, but as yet he knew nothing of God in his own experience. We see this in his confession in Bethel's cave, "Surely the LORD is in this place, and I was not aware of it" (Genesis 28:16).

We see also the lack of all filial love and confidence. "He was afraid and said, 'How awesome is this place!'" (28:17). It was a raw, unlightened, natural heart shrinking from the presence of God, knowing nothing of trust and love. But to that poor, dark, lonely heart, God came and made Himself known by that vision of divine light and revelation, which became, not only to him, but to all coming generations, a ladder reaching to heaven from the lowest, loneliest spot.

I remember well the day that I rode along the path that leads to the ruins of ancient Bethel. I stopped from time to time at the numerous caves along the road and wondered in which of them Jacob lay down with a stone for his pillow on the first night of his absence from his home. My guide pointed across the valley, and he said, "This is the cave where Jacob slept, because yonder you can see on the rocky hillside the great ledges of stone rising one above the other like mighty steps. And in the dim moonlight, you know, it seemed to Jacob like a ladder that reached in heaven." You see my guide was an accomplished higher critic. He thought he could explain the Bible without any supernatural element. I told him I knew better. The ladder Jacob saw was not that bold ledge of ascending rocks. It was that invisible stair which your faith and mine has often seen since, reaching from our helplessness to His high heaven and bringing down the angels of God on messages of help and blessing. That was the time when Jacob first met God.

There comes such an hour in every redeemed life. You had known about Jesus Christ, you had chosen Him, you had set your heart upon Him, but He had never yet become a real fact in your experience. But one night of loneliness, one hour of deep trouble, some crisis when you were forced to pray, you found God. He became revealed to you henceforth as the greatest fact in your life, the One with whom you have to do, your covenant God and Friend. He said to you as He did to Jacob: "I am with you and will watch over you wherever you go . . . I will not leave you until I have done what I have promised you" (28:15). It is yours to choose Him. It is His to make Himself known. "Let us acknowledge the LORD; let us press on to acknowledge

him. As surely as the sun rises, he will appear"
(Hosea 6:3).

Following through Years of Imperfection

In the fourth place, the God of Jacob is one who
follows His children even through years of imper-
fection and wandering while they are often far
from Him. For Jacob went forth from that Bethel
vision a new man. Jacob was a man of God but he
was still full of the old selfish, supplanting spirit.
We see him following his own devices, fighting his
own battles, intriguing with Laban and trying to
match his cunning with equal cunning. We see
him bargaining for a wife and losing in the first
transaction. We see him later getting the better of
his uncle, and finally, through deep strategy leav-
ing the land of his temporary adoption possessed
of boundless riches. Yet he was the same old Jacob
in many ways. He had asked God to prosper him
in his business contrivances and schemes. But still
it was Jacob, the worm Jacob, the selfish, supplanting Jacob. But God did not leave him all
these years. He followed him, loved him, blessed
him, prospered him, and in due time called him
back to better things.

And so, dear child of God, He has followed you
even amid your wanderings. He has not wanted
you where you were; but He has not left you
alone. As He went with Israel through the wilderness, so He has gone with you on the weary wanderings. In all your affliction He has been
afflicted, and the Angel of His Presence has saved

you and has led you all your days. Thus God still loves His imperfect children. He does not forsake them in their mistakes and follies, but He is still a God of infinite longsuffering, boundless patience and tender, fatherly pity. This should not encourage us to live short of our highest privileges, but it should lead us by grateful love to follow Him more closely and choose His highest will.

Pressures Us to Our Crisis

Then, we see in Jacob's God one who at last knew how to bring the pressure that led Jacob to the crisis of his life. The time had come for a new and deeper experience, so God led him back toward his ancient home. It is the old Jacob coming back. He is enlarged with flocks and herds and a great household, but we see Jacob all through his wise forethought, and his infinite contriving to protect his family and his flocks. When he finds his incensed brother Esau coming to meet him with an armed band, he exhausts all the resources of his skill and invention to forestall him or defend himself from him. He divides his family and his flocks into little bands so that if one is stricken the other will escape. At last he realizes how vain it all is, and he is thrown absolutely and helplessly upon the mercy and power of God.

The way narrows to a lone path where only two can walk, God and Jacob. There just across the brook Jabbok and under the solemn stars of the Orient, Jacob came face to face with the crisis of his life. He must either go down or go higher. It is either God or ruin. And so the religious instinct turns heavenward. Jacob prays as he has never prayed before.

But there is another conflict. God is wrestling with Jacob more than Jacob is wrestling with God. We are told significantly that "a man wrestled with him till daybreak" (Genesis 32:24). It was the Son of Man. It was the Angel of the Covenant. It was God in human form pressing down and pressing out the old Jacob life. And before the morning broke God had prevailed and Jacob fell with his thigh dislocated. But as he fell, he fell into the arms of God and there he clung and wrestled too until the blessing came. Then the new life was born and he arose from the earthly to the heavenly, the human to the divine, the natural to the supernatural. As he went forth that morning he was a weak and broken man. But God was there instead and the heavenly voice proclaimed: "Your name will no longer be Jacob, but Israel, because you have struggled with God and with men and have overcome" (32:28).

Beloved, this must ever be a typical scene in every transformed life. There comes a certain hour to each of us, if God has called us to the highest and best, when all the resources fail, when we face either ruin or something higher than we ever dreamed, when we must have infinite help from God. Yet before we can have it we must let something go. We must surrender completely. We must cease from our own wisdom, strength and righteousness and become crucified with Christ and alive in Him. God knows how to lead us up to this crisis and He knows how to lead us through.

Beloved, is He leading you there? Is this the meaning of your deep trial, of your difficult surrounding, of that impossible situation, or that trying place through which you cannot go without Him and yet you have not enough of Him to give you victory? Oh, turn to Jacob's God. Cast yourself helplessly at His feet. Die to your strength and wisdom and in His loving arms rise like Jacob into His strength and all-sufficiency. There is no way out of your hard and narrow place but at the top. You must get deliverance by rising higher and coming into a new experience with God. Oh, may it bring you into all that is meant by the revelation of the Mighty One of Jacob.

The Discipline of Suffering

In the sixth place we see in Jacob's God the God who knows how to finish His work by the slow discipline of suffering. That experience at Jabbok was the real crisis; but the completion of the work required the years that followed. There are some things which God can only do through time. There are processes of grace that need to be carried through long years of discipline. There is a slow fire which dissolves and consumes as no fierce furnace heat can ever do in a moment of time. There is One who sits as a Refiner and Purifier of silver through the long years, finishing His work until He can see His image in the molten metal. This is the God of Jacob. And so, through the forty years that followed, He led Jacob through the longest, slowest hardest trials. And how keen the pain! How sensitive the spirit that He touched!

So He comes to you, beloved, in the place that hurts you most. Often it is our heart's deepest affections. Rachel died; his family pride was wounded in the dishonor of his daughter; Joseph, Rachel's son, was torn from his presence amid scenes and associations of unspeakable horror. The years dragged out their slow length with that haunting shadow of suspense and agony, until at last he cried, "Everything is against me." But all the while Jacob was being burned up and God burned in. And when at last we meet him in the calm sunset of his life we hear the rash, self-confident man saying something he could not have learned otherwise. "I look for your deliverance, O LORD" (49:18). And we see the sorrow at last turned into joy. We see the shadows pass away and the rainbow arch surmount their frowning masses. We hear the evening song of a victorious life, ". . . the God before whom my fathers Abraham and Isaac walked, the God who has been my shepherd all my life to this day, the Angel who has delivered me from all harm" (48:15-16).

We see even Joseph given back and all the sorrow turned into joy while its blessed spiritual lesson remains forevermore in the transformed life of the venerable patriarch and the established saint. Thus the God of Jacob knows how to try us and how to deliver us out of trial.

Do not be surprised at the painful trial you are suffering, as though something strange were happening to you. But rejoice that you participate in the sufferings of Christ, so that you may be overjoyed when his glory is revealed. (1 Peter 4:12-13)

These have come so that your faith—of greater worth than gold, which perishes even though refined by fire—may be proved genuine and may result in praise, glory and honor when Jesus Christ is revealed. (1:7)

Using the Instrument He Prepared

The seventh point we will consider is that the God of Jacob is a God who loves to use the instrument that He has thus prepared. It was not Abraham the mighty believer. It was not Isaac, the meek and gentle son. It was Jacob, the transformed supplanter, whom God chose to be the head of Israel's tribes and the founder of the chosen people, who, on his dying bed, pronounced the prophetic blessing upon his seed which all the ages since then have been fulfilling. To this day the nation bears the name of Israel and the seed of Jacob.

And so God will take our lives when He has prepared them in proportion to what they have cost Him. The degree of power that comes out of an element is measured by the degree that goes into it. The mighty power that ran the steamer and the train came out of the coal mine. But all that power was put in the coal mine ages ago, when God burned up by fiery heat of primeval times the vast forest of vegetation that covered the world and turned them into the mines of earth. Then it went out from the mines of earth in another form of the same power.

After God has pressed into a life by long and hard processes of trial and discipline the influences of His grace and the power of His transforming Spirit, then He loves to take out of that life the same power and expend it upon others. Power can never be lost. So if we receive of God's fullness we can no more help giving it out than the sun can stop shining. And so the God of Jacob, if we will let Him have us, hold us, fill us, will surely use us. Whether it is as silent salt that penetrates the air with its wholesome savor, or the glorious light that more positively radiates over earth and sky, we will become forces for good. We will be instruments for the glory of God and the blessing of our fellowman, and all flesh will know "that I, the LORD, am your Savior, your Redeemer, the Mighty One of Jacob" (Isaiah 49:26).

CHAPTER
4

The God of Esther

*Surely your wrath against men brings
      you praise,
and the survivors of your wrath are restrained.
      (Psalm 76:10)*

*"For if you remain silent at this time, relief and
deliverance for the Jews will arise from another
place, but you and your father's family will perish. And who knows but that you have come to
royal position for such a time as this?" (Esther
4:14)*

We have been looking at the divine character
and resources as illustrated in the lives of remarkable men occupying a high place in the stage
of history and kingdom of God. We will now look
at the revelation of God as it appears in a unique
and very different situation, in the life of a lone
girl and a despised man, far removed from sympa-

41

thy and influence and called to face the most trying difficulties and the most terrific dangers. The
story of Esther tells us how God can meet such a
life and make the wrath of man to praise Him.

The Story

The story doesn't take long to tell. It is one of
the romances of the Bible. It is a chapter from the
reign of Xerxes, the rich and splendid king of Persia, whose mighty army of millions was defeated
by the brave Greeks.

The drama opens with a splendid feast costing
millions of dollars. At the height of the party the
king called for his beautiful and favorite wife to
appear before his drunken lords. She was called to
gratify their coarse curiosity by what always is to
an Eastern woman a sacrifice of modesty, the ex-
hibition of her beautiful face. Vashti refused and
was deposed from her high place and another was
sought to fill it.

In the family of an upright Jew named Mordecai,
was a beautiful maiden, his niece, Esther. To her
lot it fell in the providences of God to inherit the
crown of Vashti and to become queen of Persia.

The favorite court official of Xerxes was a
proud noble named Haman. Haman and his van-
ity were deeply wounded by the refusal of Mordecai to pay the worship and obeisance that he
claimed from the people. Mordecai disdained to
degrade himself at the feet of any man and so
Haman tried to destroy him. The plot moves on
with a dramatic force. Haman was too proud to

wreak his vengeance upon Mordecai alone. He determined upon a magnificent revenge, the destruction of Mordecai's people, the entire Jewish nation scattered throughout the empire of Persia and numbering doubtless many millions. In an evil hour he won the consent of Xerxes. A decree went forth, signed by the king's royal signet, which none could reverse, that on a certain day the whole Jewish population could be massacred under official sanction. In addition to this he planned the destruction of Mordecai himself and even went so far as to erect the gallows on which Mordecai was to be hanged.

But God's providence began to work. First it came about that Mordecai was the instrument of saving the life of the king by revealing a secret plot upon his life. After that event had long been forgotten, suddenly God laid upon the heart of the king the remembrances of Mordecai's kindness. This led Xerxes to issue a royal decree which Haman himself was compelled to carry out for a public tribute to Mordecai in the sight of the whole population and of the most distinguished character.

Mordecai did not rest in quiet inaction, but immediately called upon Esther to rise to the occasion and meet the great purpose for which God had exalted her to her high station. This would be a risk for Esther. She had not been summoned into the king's presence for many days and she felt that to venture unbidden might cost her her life. It was then that Mordecai addressed to her the stirring and solemn message of the text. "For if you remain silent at this time, relief and deliverance for the Jews will arise from another place, but you and your father's family will perish. And who knows but that you have come to royal position for such a time as this?" (Esther 4:14).

This persuaded her, and asking her uncle to help her by his prayers, she ventured into the presence of the king. God was with her. The golden scepter was stretched out and her royal lord bade her ask anything she chose up to half of the kingdom. Esther was tactful enough not to press her petition too soon but she asked the king to a banquet that day and invited Haman to accompany him. But again Esther waited another day, renewing the invitation and still waiting on God to prepare the way and show her the very moment when she was to act. At last the crisis moment came just after Mordecai had been signally honored by the public tribute ordered by the king. Haman had just returned from the hated service when he went into the presence of the king and queen at the banquet. It was then that Esther, turning indignantly upon him, demanded protection from his wickedness and cruelty for her people. Haman unwittingly in pleading for her mercy insulted her before the king. Because of this the king grew angry and ordered the immediate execution of his wicked courtier.

With her action Esther obtained not only the reversal of the decree of the massacre which as impossible under the Persian law, but the issue of another decree under the royal seal as well. From that day forward the Jews throughout the empire were permitted to defend themselves and were even invited to do so under royal approval. This turned the scale on their side and when the eventful day came their threatened destruction was turned into a universal triumph and their enemies fell before them while they had life, deliverance, honor and joy. The feast of Purim is the memorial of this great deliverance and to this day it is celebrated among the Hebrew people as one of the most joyous observances of all their sacred year.

Ten Spiritual Lessons

This romantic story is full of spiritual lessons and revelations of God.

1. God rules in the affairs of nations.

It teaches us that God rules in the affairs of nations and overrules political events for His glory and the establishment of His kingdom. Above the throne of the king of Persia was the authority of the King of kings and Lord of lords. Christ is the "head over everything for the church" (Ephesians 1:22). The government of nations and the events of providences are but the working out of God's higher will. They are the scaffolding on which He is building up His spiritual kingdom and His eternal purpose for His people. The very king of Persia arose in the fulfillment of Daniel's prophecy. The very throne of Xerxes was but a foundation on which

God had meant to build the story of Esther and her people. God used the kingdom to be a refuge for His people, a discipline for them in their sins, and an occasion for His wonderful providences in their deliverances.

2. God uses the plans of the ungodly for His purposes.

We see the plans and pleasures of the ungodly used by God for higher purposes. The costly and extravagant banquet of Xerxes, the deposition of his queen, and even his own selfish desire for the most beautiful maiden in his empire—all these became links in God's providence for bringing Esther to the front and using her for the great trust which she should afterwards fulfill in the deliverance of His people.

And so the business and the pomp and pleasure of the world are simply occasions for God to introduce the history of His own people and the working out of some greater plan. Just as the court of Persia was the home of Nehemiah and the house of Pharaoh the place for Moses to be trained, so Xerxes' palace was but a providential door through which Esther might pass upon the stage of providence and work out her beautiful and glorious career of faith and victory.

3. Our gifts, talents and stations in life are part of God's plan.

Our gifts, qualities, talents, and stations in life are all part of the divine plan and trust given us by God to be used for Him. Esther's beauty was not her own, but God's endowment. Esther's high and queenly place was not an opportunity for a selfish and splendid life, but was a door of service for God and her people. Her influence over the king was not given her that she might aggrandize her own interests and fortune, but that she might use it in time of need to help the cause of Jehovah. And so our natural qualities of person, our wealth, our social position, our plans, our public positions of power or influence—these are all sacred trusts that God has placed in our hands for us to use for Him. Of us He says as he did of Esther, "Who knows but that you have come to royal position for such a time as this?" (Esther 4:14). Beloved, are we so using them? Do we count all things His and not our own, and are we watching every opportunity to turn them to account for the purpose for which they are given us?

4. Things often occur that God will use later.

We learn from the story of Esther that God often permits things to occur and then be apparently forgotten for the purpose of using them at a later period as links in His providential plan. The little incident of Mordecai saving the life of the king which was allowed to pass by without recognition was not God's fault. But in due time the opportune moment came and it became the turning point in Mordecai's career. It aroused for him the sympathy and recognition of the king and the people and prepared him for a place of high trust that he afterwards filled. So God lets things happen in our lives, little acts of obedience, faith and sacrifice that go unrecognized. We forget all about them perhaps, but in due time the wheel of providence turns around and they come to the front and God makes them the occasion of some high calling, some marvelous opening, some grand reward.

Let us count nothing insignificant. God is working in everything and far in advance of all that we can see. Let us watch for the fulfillment of His plan and we will always have providences to watch.

5. *God often uses those who don't know Him.*

God often lays His burdens on the hearts of men who do not know Him and uses them to carry out His plans. "I summon you by name and bestow on you a title of honor, though you do not acknowledge me" (Isaiah 45:4). That was God's word to Cyrus, that mighty king who was God's direct instrument for carrying out one of His greatest plans. God used him even though Cyrus himself was an ignorant and superstitious heathen.

So too He spoke to Xerxes and made him understand His will. There was a night when the luxurious Persian king was unable to close his eyes in sleep. As he lay dozing on his bed he felt something was wrong. When the morning dawned, he sent for his counselors and had them search the records of the kingdom until they found that the faithful Mordecai had never been rewarded for his great service in saving the king's life.

What a glimpse this gives us into the mysteries of divine government. What a meaning it adds to the mighty announcement of our ascended King, "All authority in heaven and on earth has been given to me" (Matthew 28:18). He is able to move the hearts of men for our defense at His will while we calmly wait, keeping our hands off and looking to Him to work for us and to shield us with His mighty wing.

I have known an ungodly man to become so impressed that he must give a large amount for some of God's suffering children that he could not rest until the trust was discharged. Although he did it, he wondered at himself and could not explain or even justify his impulsive action. One of the largest gifts ever offered for missions in this country was a bequest made by a man who had never had any special interest in missions until his last days. He made this bequest after some friends had specially prayed that God would send help for His course. We have a God that can reach all hearts, and there are people whom we could not reach directly whom we can always touch by way of the throne.

6. *God often permits the wicked to triumph for a while.*

God often permits the wicked for a time to triumph and the cause of His people to reach a crisis of danger that almost goes too far. How imminent the peril of Esther's people! How close the coincidences! How sudden and swift the interpositions of God and the deliverance of the doomed nation.

It almost seemed as if things had gone too far. Everything was encompassed with difficulty. Only the Divine hand could avert it. But how perfectly everything fitted together. How sharply the whole drama was focused into one short day of astounding surprise! Truth indeed was stranger than fiction, and as is ever true, the story of faith is the sublimest romance of history.

Is He trying you? Are your difficulties and adversaries thickening on every side? Does it almost seem as though the promise has lingered so long that it might come too late? Trust Him. His path is in the whirlwind and the storm. The clouds are the dust of His feet. He will not let the promise fail. "Though it linger, wait for it; it will certainly come and will not delay" (Habakkuk 2:3).

7. *God's plans are prepared in advance.*

God has His plans prepared in advance of the devil's maneuvers and His instruments ready to counteract Satan's deepest designs. Zechariah tells us in one of his visions of four horns that the enemy set out to pierce God's people but four carpenters followed close behind them to fray their horns and take away their power to harm. So here while the devil had his weak and unscrupulous Xerxes ready by his rash decree to destroy a nation, God had His wise and upright Mordecai in the place of faith and influence prepared to counteract his folly. The devil had his diabolical Haman but the Lord had His Esther a little nearer the center of power to interpose just at the right moment. There are no surprises in the government of God. He is always prepared for the enemy and if we abide in Him and closely follow Him, there is no power in earth or hell that can ever harm us.

8. *God expects obedience and cooperation.*

While God is ever watching and working to defend His people and His cause, yet He expects from them their prompt, obedient and courageous cooperation in the crisis hour. There are occasions when there is nothing for us to do but wait and trust, but there are moments for prompt, wise, decisive action. When those moments come there must be no parleying and hesitation or half-heartedness.

Such a moment came to Esther when her uncle directed her to go into the presence of the king and plead for her people. It was natural for her to hesitate, but it would have been folly for her to have disobeyed. God had other agencies that He could have raised up, and, indeed, Mordecai firmly believed that deliverance and enlargement would come from some other quarter if she had failed, but she and her family would have perished.

There are times, dear friend, when you and I must speak brave words for right, must incur prejudice and misrepresentation because we stand by a cause that needs assistance. In these times the safest thing is always to be brave and true. Let us not hesitate to speak a word of vindication, to stand at the risk of interest, friendship or even life itself for the cause of truth, for the work of God. It needs much wisdom to show us just when to be still and when to act. There is a moment when the order is, "Stand firm and you will see the deliverance the LORD will bring today" (Exodus 14:13). But there is another moment when the order is, "Move on" (14:15). When that moment comes, decisive action is the only course of safety and honor.

9. *God will save us and punish the wicked.*

God not only saves us from the wicked but lets them fall into their own execution. The decree that called for the massacre of the Hebrews brought instead the destruction of their enemies. The man that was doomed to death by the conspiracy of his adversaries was lifted into the place that these very enemies had formerly held. The way of the wicked was turned upside down, and their shafts reverted upon their own heads.

It is a terrible thing to take a stand against God or His people. Christ counts the persecution of His children as His own. Our hatred and opposition to the cause of Christ and the servants of Christ are counted by the Scriptures as our fighting even against God. And it is a fearful thing to plunge against the sword of the Almighty.

Let us be careful how we touch God's anointed or wrong His servants. Such weapons will be turned against us in bitter failure and retribution. We cannot be too careful in speaking against the children of God. We are liable to be misled. Where we are not able to commend, silence is often the safest course. But they who scatter firebrands, arrows and death will find their own houses on fire and their own hearts pierced by the returning shafts.

10. *There are times of particular responsibility.*

There are crisis times in the history of individuals and religious movements and those are times of peculiar responsibility. Such a time had come in the life of Esther and on that moment converged all the significance of her life and all the preparation of God's providence in the years before.

Surely if ever there was a crisis time in the history of the world it is today. Beloved, let us remember that we, too, are come to the kingdom for such a time as this. All things are focusing into the consuming light of the world's last crisis. God has given to each of us our kingdom of opportunity, natural ability, providential environment, or spiritual endowment for the most solemn and important responsibilities and ministries. May He help us to be wholly true and "make the most of every opportunity" (Colossians 4:5).

CHAPTER
5

The God of Job

My ears had heard of you
*   but now my eyes have seen you.*
Therefore I despise myself
*   and repent in dust and ashes.*
*   (Job 42:5-6)*

The book of Job is the world's oldest poem and presents some of the profoundest spiritual teachings also presented in the book of Revelation. It is an inspired drama and its design is twofold: first, to unfold the principles of God's moral government in dealing with men; second, to show the inadequacy of human nature to stand the tests of life without a deeper and diviner spiritual life.

The Life of Job

The leading figure of the drama is a man who stands above his fellowmen in all the best qualities of human character. By the testimony of God he was a good man, the best man on earth, a man who "fear[ed] God and shun[ned] evil" (Job 1:8). He was undoubtedly a servant of God and we would call him a converted man. But he had not yet passed through the deeper experience of self-crucifixion which brings the soul into the divine nature and experience of true sanctification.

To this man God permitted the severest tests to come. The first part of the dramatic scene appears in the deep inquiries of his friends and counselors into the cause and explanation of his peculiar trial. Three men came to him, three eminent philosophers and moralists, representing all the best qualified of the wisdom of the world. Their very names are significant of the honor, the strength, the wealth, the beauty, and the wisdom of the world.

Day after day through his protracted and distracting trial they sat by his side. They talked with him, vainly trying to comfort him. They still more vainly tried to instruct him in the principles of divine government and show him that he must be guilty of some great iniquity or God would not thus afflict him. Each of them had three turns and Job in turn answered each of them three times. But when it all ended none of them was wiser than at first. Job was utterly unsatisfied with their consolations and exhortations, and dismissed them with the honest and sarcastic words: "Miserable comforters are you all!" (16:2).

They represent the world's best philosophy and wisdom, and they prove the utter inadequacy of the human mind by all its searching to "find out God."

But trial develops yet another fact, and that is the failure of Job. The good man soon broke under his terrible continued affliction, and began to vindicate himself and reflect upon God for the injustice and severity of his affliction.

Then a fourth character appeared upon the scene, Elihu, whose name signifies his direct relation to God as His servant and messenger. He came with an entirely new message, even with the inspired Word of God Himself. Twice he spoke and Job also answered him, but all his profound and deeply spiritual teaching fell in vain upon the ears of the tried and distracted sufferer. A stronger influence, a diviner touch was necessary before Job's heart would yield and his lesson be fully learned.

At last it came and it came only through the direct revelation of God Himself. After they had all spoken and Job had again and again reechoed and repeated his complaints and self-justification, God suddenly appeared upon the scene in a sublime vision of majesty and power, and spoke to him from the midst of the whirlwind. The message was in two sections interrupted by a brief pause in which Job broke down and sank to silence and submission before God's demand.

The LORD said to Job:

"Will the one who contends with the
    Almighty correct him?
Let him who accuses God answer him!"

Then Job answered the LORD:

> "I am unworthy—how can I reply to you?
> I put my hand over my mouth.
> I spoke once, but I have no answer—
> twice, but I will say no more." (40:1-5)

But God proceeded with His majestic message through the next two chapters, unfolding to Job the majesty and glory of the natural creation. He points to the forces of nature, the stars in their courses, the ordinances of heaven, the clouds and lightning, the springs of the sea, the providence that supplies the wants of every living thing, the instincts of the birds, the mighty creatures that roam in the ocean and depths of the forest. As the vision of God's majesty and glory passed before the mind of the humble and broken penitent, all Job's pride and self-vindication passed away. He cried: "My ears had heard of you but now my eyes have seen you. Therefore I despise myself/and repent in dust and ashes" (42:5-6).

The Significance of Job's Crisis

This was at length the crisis of Job's spiritual life. This was the death of self and the beginning of the life of God and from this hour the whole story turns upon its axis and the whole life and experience of Job becomes transformed. The moment he condemned himself God began to justify him. The moment he sank in the dust God began to lift him up. The moment he ceased arguing and contending with his friends and began to pray for them, God turned his captivity and brought them to bow at Job's feet and ask for his forgiveness and that he would pray for them. From that hour even his temporal circumstances were changed, his trials passed, all that he had lost was restored to him twofold. Henceforth life flowed on upon a new plane of resurrection power, glory and blessing. Let us look, therefore, more closely at this turning point, this crisis of a life, this great example which God has held out to us in the story of His ancient servant.

1. The Value of a Revelation

The words of our text remind us of the value of a revelation of divine truth. "My ears had heard of you" (42:5). This describes the revelation which comes to the outward ear and the natural intelligence which it represents. In the drama of the book of Job, Elihu represents the revelation of God's Word which comes to the ear and to the mind.

It is needless to say that the revelation of God's will and purpose is absolutely necessary and is the foundation of all deeper spiritual revelations to the soul. But at the same time, the revelation of the truth is not known without the deeper revelation of God Himself to the inner spirit by the Holy Spirit. It requires a spiritual mind to understand the teaching of the Spirit. The cold, natural intellect cannot receive the things of God by the hearing of the ear alone. Therefore, many of the brightest and profoundest minds have failed to understand the deeper teachings of the Scriptures and have even become, by their higher criticism, enemies of the Bible and misinterpreters of the volume they have professed to elucidate and explain. The greatest weakness of Christianity today arises from the fact that so many of its followers have only heard of God by the hearing of the ear.

2. *A Deeper Revelation of God*

Our text teaches us the need of a deeper revelation of God Himself. "Now my eyes have seen you" (42:5), Job cried. It is not the truth but the God of truth. It is not the book but its Author and Inspirer that we are now dealing with. The mission of the Holy Spirit is to reveal God through the truth and back of the truth to the earnest and inquiring soul. This was the experience that had come to Job and which broke his heart, humbled his pride, slew his self-sufficiency, and made room in his heart and life for God.

This has ever been the turning point of every great spiritual life. We are told that far off in Mesopotamia the God of glory appeared to Abraham (Genesis 12:7), and from that moment the whole story of faith began. It was easy for him to leave his country and his home. It was easy for him to go into an unknown future. There was One henceforth with him whom he personally knew and in whose appearance all else became as nothing. God had appeared to him.

Later another figure appears on the scene at a still greater crisis in the history of redemption. It is the great lawgiver, Moses. But the secret of Moses' life is all given in a single sentence: "He persevered because he saw him who is invisible" (Hebrews 11:27). He had met God. He always saw Him. The deepest cry of Moses' heart and life was offered later when he prayed: "Now show me your glory" (Exodus 33:18). "If your Presence does not go with us, do not send us up from here. How will anyone know that you are pleased with me and with your people unless you go with us?" (33:15-16).

The next great life that stands out in bold relief in Israel's story is David, and the one predominant and determining feature of his life was godliness. "I have set the LORD always before me" (Psalm 16:8), is the watchword of his whole experience. Isaiah's call came in that hour of which he says, "I saw the Lord seated on a throne, high and exalted" (Isaiah 6:1), and then he passed through an experience precisely the same as that of Job.

The greatest character of Scripture, the mighty Paul, started upon his new career from the moment he saw a vision of the Lord Jesus. From that hour there was one Face, one Form, one Presence, one thought that dominated his life—the vision, the presence, the will of his Master.

The greatest moment in every life is when Jesus Christ becomes actually present and intensely real and vivid in our consciousness. Beloved, has that moment come to you? Have you passed from the mere stage of intellectual knowledge of Christ to personal intimacy? Is it the historical Christ or is it the Christ of today of whom you can say as one of the devoutest of the German writers said: "It seems to me as if Jesus Christ had been crucified only yesterday."

3. *The Vision of God*

The effect of the vision of God on Job was marked and immediate. It brought about the death of self. The glare of that sunburst of divine glory blinded Job to every other light and sight of himself. All his vindications, justifications, self-complacencies were gone. In the light of God's glory Job could only see himself as worthless and utterly vile, and he longed to get out of his own sight and never see himself again. It was not merely that he took back his words and repudiated his acts, but he hated and renounced himself.

Self-denial is not giving up a few things, but it is letting self go and refusing any longer to know ourselves, to live for ourselves, or to expect any good from ourselves.

This was the effect of the vision of God upon Isaiah. When he saw Jehovah in His glory he cried, "I am ruined! For I am a man of unclean lips, and I live among a people of unclean lips, and my eyes have seen the King, the LORD Almighty" (Isaiah 6:5).

When Daniel saw this great vision he tells us, "I had no strength left, my face turned deathly pale and I was helpless" (Daniel 10:8).

This is the only way that self can ever die: a sight of Christ, and above all, the reception of

Christ to live and reign in the will, the heart, the life. That sight will drive out every rival—especially that oldest and worst rival of all, our own will, our own self-confidence, self-righteousness and self-love.

The second effect of the revelation of God was the uplifting of Job's heart to a higher place of divine life. Immediately we find him praying for his enemies. If there is one miracle greater than another it is when human hate becomes transformed into heavenly love. There is nothing so hard as to really love the people who have exasperated, tried and tormented us—especially those that have done this like Job's friends, in the name of religion. But the vision of God made Job equal to it. There came such a flood of divine life and love into his soul that colored everything henceforth with its own color. When the heart receives Christ it sees everything and everyone in the light of Christ, and it loves not as man, but as God loves.

The third effect of the revelation of God is that Job was vindicated by God Himself. Job did not need to be revenged upon the men who had wronged him. God took them in hand and sent them to make amends themselves by humble acknowledgement of their error, by sacrificing to God, and by asking Job to pray for them.

The best revenge that we can have upon the people that have done us wrong is to be the means of blessing them. When we die to self and become one with God, God makes even our enemies to be at peace with us, brings good out of evil, and turns the curse into a blessing.

> On the day I cleanse you from all your sins, I will resettle your towns, and the ruins will be rebuilt. The desolate land will be cultivated. . . . They will say, "This land that was laid waste has become like the garden of Eden." (Ezekiel 36:33-35)

God's Restoration

Finally God Himself restored to Job doubly all that he had lost before. He gave him back his health by a divine miracle and added to his years twice as many as he had had before, so that Job lived one hundred and forty years after his restoration. Probably before his life ended he had reached at least two hundred years, older even than Abraham himself.

God gave Job back his family. It is particularly mentioned that the daughters of Job were the most beautiful women in the land, and their names are all significant of the highest qualities both of person and of heart.

God gave him back his property so that he had twice as much in every kind of earthly ware as he had formerly enjoyed. He blessed Job's later years more than those in the beginning.

All this is still true: "Seek first his kingdom and his righteousness, and all these things will be given to you as well" (Matthew 6:33). It will not necessarily come to pass in this world in the life of a saint that earthly prosperity will be measured out to him in proportion to the spiritual blessing. But before the circle is completed, before the true life is finished, it will be made real, for this world is but a segment of the circle, but a chapter of the story.

It is when He comes again that all the promises of blessing that come to the consecrated soul will be fully realized and that "all these things" will be completely added. Thus "everyone who has left houses or brothers or sisters or father or mother or children or fields for [Christ's] sake will receive" not double but "a hundred times" (19:29). Then it will be true: "If we endure, we will also reign with him" (2 Timothy 2:12). Then the lives that have died to self and sin will sit with Him on His throne. They will share "the power of an indestructible life" (Hebrews 7:16). They will receive for every cross a crown, and for every weight of pain "an eternal glory that far outweighs them all" (2 Corinthians 4:17). For the little sacrifice of a surrendered life they will receive "an inheritance that can never perish, spoil or fade" (1 Peter 1:4).

CHAPTER
6

The Secret of the Vision

If only I knew where to find him;
if only I could go to his dwelling! . . .

But if I go to the east, he is not there;
if I go to the west, I do not find him.
When he is at work in the north, I do not see him;
when he turns to the south, I catch no glimpse
of him. (Job 23:3, 8-9)

This is the cry of the soul that longs for God and feels after Him if haply it may find Him. This is the deepest cry of every true spirit, the deepest need of every human life, and the greatest prayer that God can answer for a soul. For "this is eternal life: that they may know you, the only true God, and Jesus Christ, whom you have sent" (John 17:3).

How can we find God? How will He become to our consciousness more real and satisfying than any other personality and other need?

God in Nature

First, we can find God in nature.

The heavens declare the glory of God;
    the skies proclaim the work of his hands.
Day after day they pour forth speech;
    night after night they dispatch knowledge.
. . .

Their voice goes out into all the earth,
    their words to the ends of the world.
(Psalm 19:1-2, 4)

Nature alone is not able to reveal God in His gracious character as the sinful soul needs to know Him. But after we know Him from His Word, then nature is full of the most blessed illustrations of His character and the most vivid unfoldings of His love and power. And the whole creation becomes to the consecrated soul a great temple with the blue heavens for its dome, the glowing stars for its lamps of fire, the vernal earth for its emerald pavement, and the voices of the ocean, the thunder, the hum and song of the whole animated creation for its ceaseless anthem of worship and praise. There is a sense in which everything we see in this beautiful world is but a letter in the great alphabet of truth, telling of Him who

Shines in the sun,
Refreshes in the breeze,
Glows in the stars,

And blossoms in the trees.
Lives through all life,
Extends through all extent,
Spreads undivided,
Operates unspent.

I am sorry for the man who cannot see God in
every turn of the beautiful kaleidoscope of nature
and hear His voice in every note of the great organ
of this voiceless world.

God in His Word

Second we find God in His Word. Nature alone
spells out only half of the sentence and writes
upon the heavens and earth, "God is." But it
leaves an awful blank. The Bible alone can finish
the sentence and write the complete revelation,
"God is love."

The nineteenth Psalm, from which I have ear-
lier quoted, quickly passes from the natural to the
supernatural. It moves to the testimony of the
Word respecting the attributes and glory of God.
While the heavens declare His glory and the earth,
the work of His hands, it is "the law of the Lord"
that

. . . is perfect,
reviving the soul.
The statutes of the Lord are trustworthy,
making wise the simple.
The precepts of the Lord are right,
giving joy to the heart.

The commands of the LORD are radiant,
  giving light to the eyes.
The fear of the LORD is pure,
  enduring forever.
The ordinances of the LORD are sure
  and altogether righteous. (Psalm 19:7-9)

The Bible is the mirror of God. On every page we behold His glorious face. In Genesis we see Him before there was anything else to see, the supreme and solitary Being who was before all things. And then we see the teeming universe spring from His mighty creating hand, sustained by His almighty providence. The fall of man wrecks His beneficent plan, but God is still there equal to the occasion with His wonderful resources of redemption.

The story unfolds and each page shines with the presence of God. The brightest character of the antediluvian world, holy Enoch, is distinguished by the fact that he walked with God. But it is more than Enoch we see. Abraham is but a little child stepping out into the unknown, holding the hand of God.

Joseph, Moses, Joshua, Samuel, David, all represent the peculiar presence and personality of the infinite and ever-present God. The whole story of the Old Testament is a constant revelation of God amid all the changing scenes and overruling all the elements and forces of evil as well as good. The New Testament brings to us the vision of God in the face of Jesus Christ and leaves us with the

Holy Spirit as the perpetual Presence of God into the inmost heart and life of every believer.

But the God of the Bible is more than this. To believing souls He is not only God but our God. The Bible is more than a mirror. It is a love letter with your name inscribed upon it, a bankbook by which you draw from your great deposit all that it promises. The only way to make the Bible interesting is to learn to read it with your own name in it and to see in every promise a direct message for you. Would you meet God every day? Go to this precious book for a personal word morning by morning and evening by evening. You will learn to prize it, to mark it as the memorial of life's crisis hours and the history of your own experience.

God in His Providences

Third, we may find God in His providences, in the things that come to us day by day. Faith learns to recognize God in everything in some sense, even the things that come from the adversary and the hostile world. Every difficulty that meets us is a challenge to prove the resources of our heavenly Father, a vessel to hold some part of His usefulness, an occasion to prove that there is nothing too hard for Him, nothing too great for Him to undertake, nothing too little for Him to care about. Thus we find God not only in our blessings as we call them and the obvious tokens and gifts of His goodness, but in those things which are blessings in disguise. We find Him in the trials, the sorrows, the obstacles, the adverse circumstances, the very temptations and conflicts that are pressed upon us by our relentless foe, the devil.

It is possible to learn to look upon all these things as but tests that come to us from our Father's hand and opportunities of proving His love and power to help us. If we so receive them, it will come to pass that the most delightful remembrances of our lives will be the things that were most trying because they will have been transformed into blessings and triumphs. We will learn to look over the head of the devil and see God above and beyond him. By and by we will even be able to recognize him, in a sense, as our ally, as God takes our very enemy prisoner and makes him fight our battles and help to carry our burdens. This is the devil's greatest humiliation and the Lord's greatest glory.

A story is told of an old lady who was praying for bread in a time of deep distress. Some rude boys heard her prayer, and thinking they would fool her they brought a loaf of bread. Ringing her doorbell, they left it on her doorstep and slipped away. The old lady got the loaf of bread and immediately got down on her knees and thanked God for answering her prayer. This was too much for the boys and so they broke in on her and told her that she was only fooling herself, for God had not sent the bread at all but they had just brought it. "Ah," she said, "boys, I know better. It was the Lord that sent it even if it was the devil that brought it." There are so many things which the devil brings, but the child of God can see that God sent them.

Beloved, we greatly miss the discipline of life and the victories of faith if we do not watch for God in all the hard places that come to us day by day. We must learn to rise from these to our sublimest victories, to take the stones of stumbling which the devil puts in our way or throws at us and build a tower with them which reaches to heaven. If you want to meet God this week you will find a hundred places waiting where you can either surrender to the difficulty or trust your Father for victory and go forward with thankfulness and praise.

God in His People

Fourth, we can find God in His people. For the Church of Christ is His body and represents the very features of the glorious Head. It is "with all the saints" that we learn to "grasp how wide and long and high and deep is the love of Christ" (Ephesians 3:18). It is a divine art to learn to recognize the Master's face in the faces of His children and the Master's presence in the common things of every day.

It is said a distinguished artist once was employed to paint the likeness of an empress. She was far from beautiful and yet he was expected to make a beautiful portrait. He visited all parts of the empire and took the portraits of all the beautiful women in the different cities. Out of these lovely portraits he made a composite picture representing all that was most striking and beautiful in each of them. Then, by an exquisite touch of art, he put into this composite picture the expres-

sion of the countenance of the empress, that subtle
and peculiar something which belongs to a face
which represents its personality. It was the countenance of the empress, but the features were
those of all the princesses of the land.

In a higher sense the people of God are the im-
ages of the Master, and if we have both His faith
and love we will be able to find Him in His humblest disciples. How often when weary with service and even baffled at the throne of grace in
finding the very thing we needed, have we gone
forth to visit some sick and suffering child and
found at that bedside the Christ we had been looking for. There we have met in some simple expres-
sion, some incident, some word of message, some
marvelous example of patient suffering or victorious faith the very thing we needed. We have met
God. We have received the messenge wanted. We
have received more than we gave, and we have
gone forth deeply realizing that we have been with
Jesus and that we have seen the Lord.

The Ordinances of His House

Fifth, we can meet God in the ordinances of
His house. We meet Him in the worship of the
sanctuary, in the broken bread and memorial
wine, in the hour of united prayer at the altar of
public consecration, in the anointing service and
baptismal flood and in the ministries and services
of His own house. There is a peculiar sense in
which His promise is true, "Where two or three
come together in my name, there I am with them"

(Matthew 18:20). Let us not make the mistake of forsaking the assembling of ourselves together or lightly esteeming the sanctuary and its services, for while God is present in the hearts and homes of His people, yet He loves the gates of Zion more than all the dwellings of Israel.

The Secret Place and Inner Vision

Sixth, we can meet God in the secret place of the holy heart and the inner vision of the waiting spirit. This is God's favorite temple. While heaven is His throne and earth His footstool, His chosen sanctuary is the humble and contrite heart where He loves to come to bring revival. "I live in a high and holy place, but also with him who is contrite and lowly in spirit, to revive the spirit of the lowly and to revive the heart of the contrite" (Isaiah 57:15). God is always waiting to meet the devout spirit in the inner chamber of the soul when we come by the new and living Way in the name of Jesus.

But there are some things that we must remember and do if we would really meet God in the secret place of the soul.

We must have the open face. "With unveiled faces [we] all reflect the Lord's glory" (2 Corinthians 3:18). Many things may intercept the vision. One of them is the love of the world. The heart that is intensely fixed on earthly pleasure and worldly delights is incapable of seeing God.

The mighty telescope of the Lick Observatory had to be planted five thousand feet above the sea to lift it out of the mists of the lower air and bring it into the unobstructed vision of the heavenly worlds. Down on the plains of Sodom, Lot had no vision of God, but on the heights of Bethel, Abraham with nothing on earth but God to care for, received the covenant promise and the heavenly vision.

Again, the cares of the world, the anxieties of life are just as powerful to hinder the vision of God. There are many reading these lines who are so worried and distracted by a thousand earthly perplexities and troubles that their hearts are not at leisure to fix their eyes upon Jesus and behold the vision of His love. One look at Him, one sight of His almighty care would take away all your anxieties and give you "the peace of God, which transcends all understanding" (Philippians 4:7). Oh, look up from your cares with open face and hear Him say, "Cast your cares on the LORD and he will sustain you" (Psalm 55:22).

Again, the fault may be some grosser sin. A heart steeped in earthly passion and unholy thought, imaginations, desires, purposes full of hatred, full of bitterness or full of impure desire, can never see God. "Without holiness no one will see the Lord" (Hebrews 12:14). "Blessed are the pure in heart, for they will see God" (Matthew 5:8).

We need not only the open face but the open ear, for God wants to speak to us, and He will not speak unless we are willing to listen. And so we find old Habakkuk saying, "I will stand at my watch and station myself on the ramparts; I will look to see what he will say to me, and what answer I am to give to this complaint" (Habakkuk 2:1). He was ready to hear and therefore God had something to say. He expected that he might be reproved, instead he received messages of promise that became the keynotes of faith to the Church of God for all the coming ages. God will speak to us if we will hearken and He will always speak some word of love.

We need the open heart for He has said, "Here I am! I stand at the door and knock. If anyone hears my voice and opens the door, I will come in and eat with him, and he with me" (Revelation 3:20). God is waiting not only to speak to us but to sit down and feast with us. He wants to bring His heavenly banquet for our supply and taste of our poor gifts and eat with us as well as have us eat with Him. But we must open the door. The heart must be yielded. The affections must be opened without reservation to the inmost depths of our being.

We must have the obedient and responsive will. The apostle said to King Agrippa, "I was not disobedient to the vision from heaven" (Acts 26:19). God comes not only to tell us things but to have us do them. His visitation and messages are for a practical purpose, and He expects a practical response. Have we already obeyed what we know? Are we willing if He should meet us this day to gladly respond and say, "Lord, I will go. Speak, Lord for Your servant hears"? He came to little Samuel of old because He knew that Samuel would obey Him. He will come to you if He can find an open face, and open heart and an obedient will.

Finally, God shows us the vision of His grace and glory that we may take all He shows us and claim all He reveals. "All the land that you see," He said to Abraham, "I will give to you" (Genesis 13:15). "We have . . . received . . . the Spirit who is from God," said the apostle. Then he adds as an echo of the same truth "that we may understand what God has freely given us" (1 Corinthians 2:12). We know them first by the revelation of the Spirit and then we take them by the appropriating act of faith.

So He is waiting today to show us the vision of His infinite grace and power and then to give us all He shows us. Lift up your eyes, beloved, and look far and wide and long and steadily. Take it all in, for all that you can see God will give you. Look out upon the hard places of your life and behold Him waiting to transform them into victories. Take in the whole circumference of His resources and promises and then say, "all are mine."

It is as if a father should take his favorite child through some beautiful place and ask her to inspect and admire its treasures of taste and beauty and, after she had feasted her eyes upon it and expressed her admiration of its loveliness, he should hand her the key and say, "My darling child, all this is yours." And so He is saying to us, "All . . . that you see I will give to you" (Genesis 13:15). Let us look, let us take. Then let us use the fullness and the blessing all for Him and for those to whom He has made us witnesses and trustees of His grace and blessing.

Scripture Index

Simpson Titles

Books by A.B. Simpson

The Best of A.B. Simpson
    (compiled by Keith M. Bailey)
The Christ in the Bible Commentary—Six Volumes
Christ in the Tabernacle
Christ in You
The Christ of the Forty Days
The Cross of Christ
Danger Lines in the Deeper Life
Days of Heaven on Earth (devotional)
Divine Emblems
The Fourfold Gospel
The Gentle Love of the Holy Spirit
The Gospel of Healing
The Holy Spirit—Power From on High
The Land of Promise
      (commentary on the Song of Songs)
A Larger Christian Life
The Life of Prayer
The Lord for the Body
Loving as Jesus Loves
Missionary Messages
The Names of Jesus
Portraits of the Spirit-filled Personality
Practical Christianity
Seeing the Invisible
Serving the King
The Spirit-filled Church in Action
The Supernatural
Walking in Love

When God Steps In
When the Comforter Came
Wholly Sanctified
The Word Made Flesh
        (commentary on the Gospel of John)

Booklets by A.B. Simpson

A.W. Tozer and A.B. Simpson on Spiritual Warfare
Christ Our Sanctifier: A.B. Simpson on the Deeper Life
Gifts and Grace
Hard Places: Stepping Stones to Spiritual Growth
Higher and Deeper: A Roadmap for Christian Maturity
Himself
Is Life Worth Living? A Study in Ecclesiastes
Paul: Ideal Man, Model Missionary
Thirty-One Kings: Victory Over Self

Books about A.B. Simpson

All for Jesus (History of The Christian and Missionary Alliance), by Robert Niklaus et al
The Baptism of the Holy Spirit: The Views of A.B. Simpson and His Contemporaries, by Richard Gilbertson
Body and Soul: Evangelism and the Social Concern of A.B. Simpson, by Daniel J. Evearitt